To my nieces Clea and Salome Molano, my nephew Aoteng Lu, my good friend Barney Tennison and my little adoptive sister Marisol Pengely. Thanks for sharing some school holidays with me and the kiwi over the years. This book is dedicated to the children you were, and the adults you are becoming. – IC

To John McLennan, who helped 'kiwi recovery' along those first important steps. – RM

First published in 2011 by New Holland Publishers (NZ) Ltd
Auckland • Sydney • London • Cape Town

www.newhollandpublishers.co.nz

218 Lake Road, Northcote, Auckland 0627, New Zealand
Unit 1, 66 Gibbes Street, Chatswood, NSW 2067, Australia
86–88 Edgware Road, London W2 2EA, United Kingdom
80 McKenzie Street, Cape Town 8001, South Africa

Copyright © 2011 in text: Isabel Castro
Copyright © 2011 in photography: Rod Morris except as credited below
Copyright © 2011 New Holland Publishers (NZ) Ltd
Isabel Castro has asserted her right to be identified as the author of this work.

ISBN: 978 1 86966 292 9

Publishing manager: Christine Thomson
Editor: Matt Turner, Wooden Shed
Design: Cheryl Rowe

Front cover: North Island brown kiwi chick.
Back cover: top: Female great spotted kiwi; bottom: North Island brown kiwi.
Title page: Great spotted kiwi.

A catalogue record for this book is available from the National Library of New Zealand.

10 9 8 7 6 5 4 3 2 1

Colour reproduction by Pica Digital Pte Ltd, Singapore
Printed by Times Offset (M) Sdn Bhd, Malaysia, on paper sourced from sustainable forests.

Photography/artwork: All images copyright Rod Morris with the exception of the bottom image on page 13, courtesy of Tony and Jenny Enderby, and page 31, courtesy of Susan Cunningham.

Fiordland tokoeka chick.

CONTENTS

Fiordland's glacial valleys are the habitat for Fiordland tokoeka kiwi.

INTRODUCTION

For New Zealanders, the word kiwi has many meanings. Principally it evokes a feeling of self and home, because since World War Two it has been used to refer to the people of this land. Kiwi, however, is the name that was given by the Maori to an unusual nocturnal, ground-dwelling bird.

The words *unique*, *strange* and *odd* are often associated with kiwi, because kiwi are so different from us that it is hard to study them – and when we do so, it is difficult to explain what they do and why. Early Maori also thought of the kiwi as a strange animal and decided it was a favourite of Tane, the god of the forest. When European scientists first saw a kiwi specimen, they assumed these unfamiliar birds were related

The first illustration of a kiwi by a European was painted in 1813 by Richard Nodder, who had never seen a live bird.

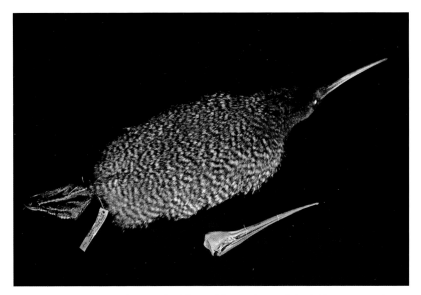

It is easy to see how skins like this, trussed and flattened for easy shipping, led early European naturalists into confused notions of what kiwi really looked like.

to penguins, perhaps because of the lack of long wings; that is why in early illustrations kiwi are drawn in unnaturally erect postures. The error occurred because they saw not a live kiwi, but skins taken back to various museum collections. Kiwi were so different to other birds described so far that the scientists of the time made mistakes when describing their anatomy. For instance, for many years people thought kiwi did not have an uropygial or preen gland; this gland is found in most birds (kiwi included), near the base of the tail, and secretes an oily substance that the bird transfers to its plumage with the use of its beak. Because kiwi lack a conventional tail, scientists simply weren't looking in the right place. (The kiwi's preen gland is actually very large.)

That said, the kiwi are a group of truly strange birds by today's standards. They are nocturnal, flightless insectivores (feeders on invertebrates) that use cavities as roosts. Their offspring hatch with adult plumage, and kiwi have the lowest metabolic rate of any bird so far measured. Two of the five kiwi species exhibit sex role reversal – dads behave like mums – and although this is not unheard of in birds, it is nonetheless rare (indeed, it is rare in the entire animal kingdom). Kiwi have a well-developed sense of smell (although new research shows this to be less rare in birds than was once thought) and a large brain, comparable to parrots' brains. Their incubation period is notably long (as with other birds, such as the albatrosses, that lay large eggs relative to adult body size). This book describes all the features that make the kiwi the wonderful bird it is, and its conservation plight, using the most up-to-date published information. I have tried to clarify the lore associated with kiwi and to be critical of our hard-gained knowledge so far. I hope that after reading this book you can *feel* kiwi and *experience* the world in a completely new way, a more *kiwi* way.

In North Island brown kiwi, incubation is typically undertaken by the male alone; however, we now know this is not the case with other kiwi species.

TOOLS TO STUDY KIWI

An antenna attached to a receiver allows this researcher to find great spotted kiwi tagged with radio transmitters living on the forested slopes above Arthur's Pass township.

For many years, scientists gained little more than brief glimpses into the kiwi's behaviour. The kiwi became a bird of legend, folklore and partial truths, and for this reason care should be taken when interpreting old tales about it. In the last 30 years or so, however, the systematic study and monitoring of kiwi populations in the wild has become possible thanks to available and affordable modern equipment, such as infrared video recording, miniaturised radio transmitters and remote sound recording. Although the emphasis has been on using some of these tools in an effort to recover kiwi populations, there have been some initiatives in the study of various aspects of kiwi biology, and researchers have used all available tools to this end.

Kiwi behaviour is being studied with the help of radio transmitters, which are attached to the tibia of the bird. Each transmitter is tuned to a unique frequency that can be detected only by a paired receiver, which is taken into the field by a researcher to track the location of specific birds. In addition, there is now access to 'smart' transmitters, which may contain data loggers that can record information on particular behavioural patterns, or which emit different signals depending on a bird's activity. This makes it possible to record specific behaviours – such as when a particular male begins incubation, or when chicks hatch – without ever seeing the birds. Thanks to the use of transmitters, we have learnt a great deal about kiwi movements, breeding methods and habitat utilisation.

A radio transmitter is attached to a great spotted kiwi's leg. Each transmitter emits a unique signal that can be located using a receiver and a directional antenna.

HOW MANY BIRDS TO STUDY?

Something of great importance when studying specific aspects of animals' lives is the number of individuals that we sample in a given place. As researchers, we want to ensure that what we see an animal doing is representative of their group, or their species, as a whole. Generally, a larger number of individuals will provide a truer picture than a small number. However, when conducting a study we are restricted in terms of our time and costs. For example, the radio transmitters we use when studying kiwi cost approximately $400 each (in 2010), and their batteries need to be changed annually at a cost of around $200 per transmitter. So it is expensive to study kiwi and this clearly limits the number of birds that can be included in a given project. When using a small sample of animals in our studies we need to be extremely critical of the results and remain cautious of generalisations. Keep this in mind when you read studies on kiwi.

Radio transmitters allow researchers to track the whereabouts of individual birds – in this case a pair of great spotted kiwi.

A North Island brown kiwi emerges from its burrow at dusk.

THE KIWI FAMILY TREE

The big picture

To trace the roots of the kiwi family tree, we must look back through the fossil record to the very source of the class Aves (the birds). Most scientists agree that all birds evolved from the subclass Neornithes (meaning 'new birds'), which in turn evolved from a common ancestor among the theropod dinosaurs. The Neornithes roamed the earth as early as 145 million years ago, in the early Cretaceous Period (although there is much debate on this date). Around 65 million years ago at the K-Pg boundary (the end of the Cretaceous and start of the Paleogene), the earth experienced a mass extinction of species, among them the terrestrial dinosaurs. A part of one dinosaur group survived: the avian dinosaurs, or birds.

Today there are two major groups of birds. These are the Palaeognathae and Neognathae superorders, which appear to have separated at some point between 120 and 80 million years ago (see Figure 1, page 11).

Kiwi ancestors belonged to the Palaeognathae, together with a number of other species of flightless birds that have been known collectively as the ratites, and another group of birds, the tinamous. Palaeognaths are characterised by having a palate resembling that of reptiles, in contrast to

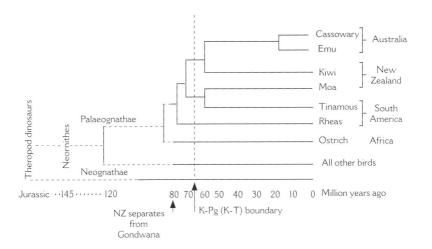

Figure 1: Evolution of birds from theropod dinosaurs, their separation into palaeognaths and neognaths, and detailed relationships between the members of the Paleognathous superorder for which we have data. Blue dotted lines represent unknown exact dates for events. Black dotted line represents a non-scale period of time. Source: various sources.

Kiwi are only distantly related to moa. This is the remarkable dried head of an upland moa (Megalapteryx didinus), *originally found near Queenstown, and now in the British Museum.*

neognaths, which have a so-called 'bird palate'. Palaeognaths also have a flat sternum (breastbone), usually without a keel, which is the ridge of bone that in flying birds serves as an attachment point for the pectoral muscles. The pectorals of palaeognaths are generally underdeveloped. This lack of strength in the chest area is associated with poor flying ability or even flightlessness; more practically, it is the reason why when handling kiwi one must take care not to hold the body tightly or the bird will be starved of breath and die. Ratites lack flight feathers, and they have a rudimentary or

The articulated skeleton of a giant moa (Dinornis robustus) *in a cave near Karamea.* Dinornis *may have been the tallest bird that ever lived – females stood 3.6 m tall and weighed up to 240 kg.*

Cassowaries (Casuaris casuaris) *are large flightless birds of the north-eastern rainforests of Australia, and New Guinea. Recent research suggests that they and the emu are the closest living relatives of kiwi.*

absent pygostyle (the 'parson's nose' or tail-bone), which explains why kiwi look so rounded.

The ratites include the extinct elephant bird (from Madagascar), the ostrich (Africa), two species of rhea (South America), the emu, three living and one extinct species of cassowary (Australia), 11 extinct species of moa, and five species of kiwi (New Zealand). The tinamous comprise about 47 species of turkey-like birds from Central and South America. While there has been little argument over which species belong to the tinamou group, the ratites seem to be a random group of species that have been classed together simply because they share features associated with the evolution of flightlessness.

All molecular analyses confirm that the kiwi lineage is more closely related to Australia's emus than to New Zealand's moa.

A red-winged tinamou (Rhynchotus rufescens) *dust-bathing. Despite their unlikely appearance, these turkey-like birds from South America have been found to be close genetic relatives of New Zealand's extinct moa.*

It was once thought the ratites and tinamous came from different ancestors because of their habits: while the ratites are flightless, tinamous can fly, albeit not very well. But recent genetic work suggests they belong to the same family branch and share a close ancestor. In this new picture, an ancestral palaeognathous bird gave rise first to the ancestors of the ostrich, and then to the ancestors of all other current ratites and tinamous. The genetic analysis further suggests that the Australian and New Zealand groups are closer to the tinamous, having shared a common ancestor, while the rhea sits on its own family branch. The moa and the tinamous are the closest genetic relatives, and they are believed to share a common ancestor with the kiwi, emu and cassowary (see Figure 1, page 11). As the word 'ratite' refers to species based on arbitrary morphological features that are not supported by molecular studies, the word can now be dropped in favour of palaeognath, which includes flying and flightless species. One observation that remains constant in all molecular analyses is that the kiwi lineage is most closely related to the emu/cassowary lineage, and not to the other group of New Zealand palaeognaths, the moa.

How did the kiwi end up in New Zealand?

There are two quite different explanations for how kiwi found themselves on this remote land mass amid the South Pacific that we call New Zealand.

Taking into account the current whereabouts of the other living palaeognaths in the southern continents, the traditional explanation supposed that a flightless ancestor of the group had become widespread through the ancient supercontinent Gondwana before it began to break up around 140 million

Kiwi are perfectly happy to enter water and cross rivers in their territories. Molecular evidence suggests the ancestors of kiwi either flew, swam or island-hopped to New Zealand.

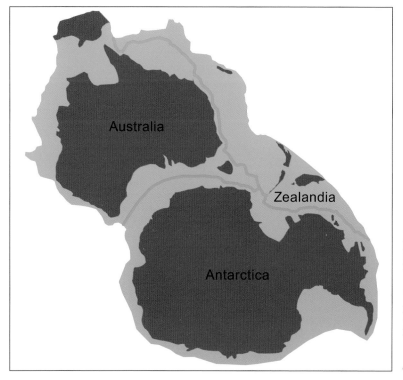

Source: Nick Mortimer/GNS Science.

Figure 2: A map of the supercontinent of Gondwana, as it was about 100 million years ago. Present day land masses and continental shelves are dark and light green. The blue lines indicate where the Gondwana land mass split apart 80 million years ago.

years ago, and that later, after continental separation (see Figure 2), the evolution of each species took place. This is known as the *vicariance biogeography hypothesis*, and it is used in textbooks around the world to explain the presence of ratites in such far-flung continents as South America, Africa, Australia and Zealandia. If this version of the story were true, a kiwi ancestor would have walked into New Zealand before 80 million years ago from the land mass we now know as Australia, and kiwi would be a very old group.

According to molecular genetic evidence, however, the separation of the various ratite groups occurred much more recently, supporting an alternative hypothesis. It states that ancestors of ratites (including kiwi) flew, swam or island-hopped into their current locations after the extinction of the non-avian dinosaurs. In the absence of many of their

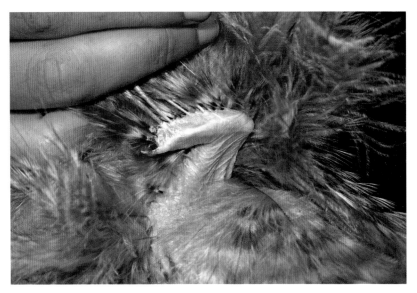

The tiny wings of the great spotted kiwi are only about the length of a matchstick. Nevertheless, the ancestors of modern kiwi may have flown to New Zealand, and evolved flightlessness much later.

dinosaur competitors and predators, palaeognath ancestors occupied some of the vacant niches and evolved flightlessness. Interestingly, fossilised palaeognath relatives have also been found in the northern hemisphere, and their existence may revolutionise our understanding of the kiwi family tree in the future.

Kiwi family relationships

Based on recent DNA analysis, five species of kiwi are currently recognised, and all are placed in the genus *Apteryx* (see Figure 3, page 18). This word, from the Greek meaning 'without wings', refers to the fact that kiwi have tiny wings. Two of the species, the great spotted kiwi (*Apteryx haastii*; South Island) and little spotted kiwi (*Apteryx owenii*; South Island and North Island), are intuitively easy to recognise because they differ greatly in size and plumage. The other three species are brownish-coloured, and to our eyes they all look very similar. These are the brown kiwi (*Apteryx mantelli*; North Island), tokoeka (*Apteryx australis*; Fiordland, Stewart Island and central South Island) and rowi (*Apteryx rowi*; northern South Island and in the past, before it became extinct there, southern North Island). In the future, genetic data might be used to further subdivide the current brown kiwi and tokoeka classification. The DNA analysis suggests, for instance, that brown kiwi from the Coromandel, Northland, eastern North Island and western North Island may be four different groups. Likewise Haast, northern Fiordland, southern Fiordland and Stewart Island tokoeka all have differences in their genetics and may end up as subspecies.

Great spotted kiwi.

Brown kiwi.

Fiordland tokoeka.

Little spotted kiwi.

Haast tokoeka.

Stewart Island tokoeka.

Female rowi.

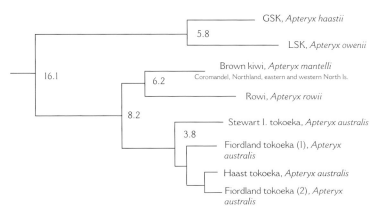

Figure 3: Phylogenetic tree showing the relationships between the different types of kiwi we have today. Source: Haddrath and Baker 2001. GSK = great spotted kiwi; LSK = little spotted kiwi.

The numbers seen at the nodes where the species or groups separate correspond to the amount of time (in millions of years) since the separation of the groups. For example, the ancestors of brown kiwi separated from those of rowi 6.2 million years ago.

A Fiordland tokoeka chick in the nest.

THE KIWI:
AN OUTLIER

An honorary mammal or dinosaur descendant?

Some of the kiwi's odd characteristics may seem more mammal-like than bird-like and have prompted some people to describe the kiwi as an 'honorary mammal'. This phrase is, however, both misleading and inaccurate. It probably reflects the fact that when most people think of 'typical' birds, they bring to mind species in the passerine (perching bird) order, such as the sparrow or blackbird. But while passerines comprise around 6000 of the 10,000 or so bird species known, there are a further 23 bird orders, many of which exhibit parallels with the unusual characteristics of kiwi. More importantly, it was only when the non-avian dinosaurs became extinct that the ecological niches (roles) now referred to as *mammalian* became available to modern reptiles, birds and mammals. Actually, bird ancestors were two-legged, terrestrial, agile runners, and were carnivorous or omnivorous – very much like kiwi. So, if we want to explain the odd characteristics of kiwi we must examine their ancestors and the kiwi's current niche.

So what are these so-called mammal-like features? Take, for instance, the plumage. Kiwi feathers resemble hair more than your typical feather.

A close-up of a brown kiwi's feathers reveals their hair-like similarities.

In some kiwi species, the feathers are a little stiff at the tips and they feel rather like human hair that contains a bit too much hair gel. Kiwi share this trait with other members of the palaeognath group: the ostrich, rhea, emu and cassowary all have feathers that lack barbs and thus resemble hair. A kiwi also has facial bristles, which makes you think of cat's whiskers. But again, bristles are not unique: they feature among owls, flycatchers and several other bird species. Kiwi have retained two functional ovaries (most birds have lost the right ovary as a trade-off for a light flying weight), and are sometimes listed as the only birds in which this occurs; but in fact paired functional ovaries are also present in some raptors including sparrowhawks, hawks and falcons. Then there is the resting body temperature of a kiwi, which at 38 °C was thought to be closer to that of mammals (37 °C) than other birds (40 °C). However, a recent review of studies has revealed that other groups of birds, including the ostrich and cassowary, as well as petrels and penguins, all have resting body temperatures of 38 °C or lower. The average resting body temperature of a bird has been calculated at 38–39 °C, and the active body temperature at 39.3–41.6 °C; the ranges are due to variations in body weight and flying ability (lower temperatures are found in large flightless species like kiwi). In mammals, these temperatures average 37 °C and 39 °C respectively and weight is not relevant to body temperature.

Some of the other so-called mammal-like features are adaptations to the kiwi's niche, which

Weighing 300 g or more, the kiwi's egg is enormous relative to its body size.

is that of a nocturnal insectivore. Kiwi have adapted to this niche by displaying a reliance on non-visual senses: the very small eyes, the long bill with nostrils at its tip (all other living birds have the nostrils at the base of the bill) and the large earholes. Some mammals that occupy a nocturnal insectivore niche also possess similar adaptations: for example, shrews, moles, hedgehogs and tenrecs. (This is an excellent example

Kiwi's nocturnal, insectivore behaviour involves searching around in dense vegetation late at night like this western brown kiwi.

of what scientists refer to as convergent evolution, in which unrelated organisms show similar adaptations to the same challenges.) One thing is for certain, though: compared with the rest of the world, New Zealand has long been a land mass almost entirely lacking in native terrestrial mammals, and this has had a significant effect on the evolutionary history of its native birds.

There is still much debate over what vertebrate species were in New Zealand when it separated from Gondwana about 83 million years ago (see Figure 2, page 15), and which arrived afterwards and when. But in any case, at the point of separation from the other land masses there were very few mammal species in the world, and those that existed were only the size of mice and voles. Dinosaurs, reptiles, amphibians and birds were the most abundant land vertebrates, and one way or other these are the groups that shaped the evolution of New Zealand's wildlife. Because New Zealand was a group of small islands, the number and density of species were low in comparison with larger, less fragmentary land masses. The extinction of the dinosaurs opened up new niches for other animals; over most of the planet, the mammals occupied these niches, while in New

A rowi, or Okarito brown kiwi, pauses to listen to the sounds of the forest and scent the night air, before moving away from the safety of its burrow to forage in the dark (above). A young Haast tokoeka is hiding deep in an underground burrow by day (opposite).

Relying mainly on a sense of hearing, touch and smell, a Stewart Island tokoeka wanders the beaches of its homeland in the dark.

Zealand it was the birds. Each newly available niche presented challenges that could be dealt with only by possessing specific characteristics. (For example, to occupy a nocturnal niche an animal's survival depends on its ability to navigate and to find partners and food in near or total darkness.) Accordingly, native New Zealand birds came to occupy those niches through a process of selection that favoured what have become, for the most part, very unbirdlike characteristics. That helps explain why today New Zealand is home to an unusually high number of bird species that are nocturnal, ground-dwelling, flightless, drab in coloration, and large in size. And, arguably, in no other native New Zealand bird species are all of these characteristics so concentrated as they are in the kiwi.

People say that the best way to understand somebody is to put yourself into their shoes. One of my students and colleagues, Susan Cunningham, wrote the following in her thesis:

> Humans rely predominantly on vision in our day-to-day lives. For us, it is hard to imagine living in a world which is not experienced primarily by how things look, but instead by how things feel, sound or smell. Even our colloquialisms about perception tend to be visually biased (for example, we

all hold different *outlooks* on life, *view* things from different perspectives, and yet attempt *to see eye-to-eye*). Studying animal species in which vision is not the dominant sense in all situations is like opening a window into another world – it gives us access to a completely different *point of view*.

For a sense of how kiwi live, try going out into a forested place, or even your garden, at night. Turn off all the lights and wait for five or 10 minutes until your eyes have adjusted. Then imagine what it would be like to walk or run, to find your friends or family, to come back home after walking for several kilometres, to find food. Kiwi are not only nocturnal, but also live on the ground. Light at this level of the forest is usually very low and even specialised eyes cannot function under such conditions. Kiwi seem to have resolved the problem of poor visibility by relying on other sensory systems. Standing out there in the dark, the first thing you'll notice is that hearing becomes important. So, too, does touch, which enables you to feel your way about and even to distinguish the shapes of objects. Finally, your sense of smell will become keener. Taken together, these sensory stimuli will give you an *insight* into how a kiwi connects with its world.

Sir David Attenborough watches a Stewart Island tokoeka foraging on sand-hoppers during filming for the television series Life of Birds. *While the tokoeka is capable of locating its food in the dark, humans need to carry torches.*

The kiwi brain

Bird brains are very different from mammal and reptile brains. It is thought that the limitations in weight imposed by flight have kept brain weight lower, and overall size smaller, in birds than in similar-sized mammals. However, birds and mammals encounter broadly similar life challenges, so it would be logical to expect that birds require similar brain capacities. Indeed, in the last few years much has been learnt about bird brains – for instance, that they are able to develop cognitive behaviours comparable to those of mammals and do not rely solely on instinct for their life skills as was previously thought.

Recently, a Northland researcher, Jeremy Corfield, and his collaborators studied the kiwi brain and found it to be surprisingly large for a palaeognathous bird, being about the size of a parrot's brain. In fact, the kiwi has a much larger brain in relation to its body size than any of its close relatives. The enlargement is mostly in the area of the brain that handles the integration of information and general cognition, including learning. The researchers suggested that this enlargement is associated with the kiwi's dependence on non-visual senses.

Great spotteds, like all kiwi, have much larger brains than any of their close relatives. The enlargement is mainly to the area of the brain associated with information processing, recognition and learning – all thought to be associated with a kiwi's dependence on non-visual information.

Eyes and vision

Kiwi are, of course, not the only birds adapted for nocturnal living. Owls' eyes, for example, function in very low light levels and provide excellent binocular vision, which in some species allows for depth perception (enabling the bird to judge the distance of an object – such as a tree, or a mouse). Compared with the eyes of diurnal birds, those of typical nocturnal birds are large relative to body size, have larger pupil apertures and are equipped with a larger number and larger size of light receptors in the retina. In particular, they contain more rods, which are light receptors specialised for low light levels. In short, the typical 'night vision' eye gathers as much light as possible.

The eyes of nocturnal birds like owls (above), are large and have adaptations to enable them to collect as much light as possible and see in near darkness. A kiwi is not as reliant on visual clues. Its eyes (below) are small in comparison, but a kiwi's external earholes, located just behind the eyes, are enormous.

So how does the kiwi compare with other nocturnal birds? The most noticeable difference is the very small eye size. This, together with a greatly reduced field of vision and associated areas of the brain, suggests that kiwi vision is poor and thus not as important as other senses (see panel, page 32). Indeed, the kiwi's field of vision is the smallest of any bird studied thus far. The

location of a kiwi's eyes low in the face means that it cannot see above the head as other birds do. Kiwi binocular vision is also limited to a very slender field directly in front of the face. The bill tip falls outside this field and so is invisible to the bird, which therefore cannot use vision as a guide when foraging. However, the kiwi retinal structure indicates specialisations for seeing in dim light. Overall, kiwi probably can see only gross details of features at night, comparable to what we can see in the same situation. Two close relatives of the kiwi, the ostrich and emu, have large eyes and very well-developed visual systems, suggesting that kiwi ancestors relied

Little spotted kiwis' eyes, like those of all kiwi, are small relative to the size of their bodies, and their location low on the side of the head results in a small field of vision.

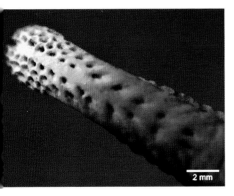

Pitting on the final 5 mm of the top mandible of a kiwi bill. The pits are filled with tissue containing nerve endings specialised in receiving pressure and vibration signals.

on vision more than their descendants do today. And during the course of evolution, natural selection favoured birds that were able to use senses other than vision on moonless forest nights, resulting in the fascinating bird we have today: a nocturnal, ground-living insectivore.

The bill-tip organ

The kiwi is well known for its habit of probing the ground in search of food, but the long bill is far more sophisticated than it might appear. One of the bill's most intriguing characteristics is the location of the nostrils at the tip. If we add this to the knowledge that large areas of the kiwi brain are dedicated to the sense of smell, it bears comparison to other nocturnal animals that rely on smell – a hedgehog or a gecko, for instance. In 2007, our group discovered another unusual feature: a so-called bill-tip organ containing what might be described as a sixth sense – a kind of 'remote touch' facility. The organ itself is located in the last five millimetres or so of the bill and it consists of heavy pitting of the bone, reminiscent of honeycomb. Each of the tiny holes in this honeycomb is filled with tissue containing specialised groups of cells called the Herbst corpuscles. The Herbst corpuscles are part of the nervous system and their role is to receive and relay information about vibration or pressure changes in the environment – in particular, the seismic waves or vibrations produced by prey moving underground.

There is still much to learn about the exact way the bill-tip organ works, but I will describe one way we think it might. When a kiwi forages, it touches the ground with the tip of the bill for a few seconds with each step. These periods of contact may enable it to sense whether prey is moving underground. Once it detects vibrations, the kiwi stops and touches the ground repetitively in various places until it gets a feel for the location of the prey, then pushes its beak into the ground to catch the prey, which may well be buried some way beneath the surface. Kiwi are not the only birds that use this type of sensory organ to find hidden prey; some species of shorebird, such as the dunlin, sandpiper and red knot, do so too, as do some ibis.

The world of smell

For a long time it was assumed that birds were anosmic (unable to detect odours). It is now known, however, that they can recognise odours and apply them in a wide range of activities, from identifying their nest and others of their species – as is the case in some petrels – to finding food or navigating.

Indeed, kiwi are known for their highly developed sense of smell. It has been well documented (in captivity, at least) that kiwi can find their food using this sense alone. Kiwi also have a number of olfactory receptor genes (for the production of molecules that allow an individual to perceive odours), and these are comparable to the numbers found in mammals. One of the reasons why birds were thought to be anosmic is that smelling behaviours had not been observed. Recent studies with kiwi, however, have described behaviours

A young North Island brown kiwi using the full length of its bill to reach prey hidden underground.

A brown kiwi foraging for prey under water may benefit from having a bill-tip organ sensitive to vibrations made by prey moving in the water.

related to the investigation of odours. For example, kiwi make two sorts of noises: a *sniff* and a *snort*. (Note that these terms only describe the sound; birds are technically incapable of sniffing in the manner of a mammal.) The *sniff* sound is accompanied by a series of movements that are thought to help birds get in contact with the source of smell (see Figure 4, page 31). The *snort* sound may have two purposes. One is to clean the nostrils after

Kiwi have excellent hearing and stop whatever they are doing and lift their heads in the direction of unusual sounds.

probing into the soil; the other is to spread nasal drip down the long bill to allow smells to dissolve into it before bringing them back up to the olfactory concha to be detected and analysed.

In a third smell-related behaviour, which we call *bill hover*, a kiwi makes a tapping motion in the air or just holds the bill tip over a small area of the ground without ever touching it. We think this behaviour is used to obtain information about scents on the ground left by prey, other kiwi, or other animals. This is in no way a far-fetched idea: kiwi faeces (see panel, page 32), which are highly scented, contain chemical compounds which may release information that can be interpreted by other kiwi. Current research on kiwi olfaction is seeking answers to a host of fascinating questions. Under what circumstances do kiwi use this sense, and how do they use it? What do kiwi do when confronted with scents of other kiwi … or with non-kiwi scents? Where does that characteristic kiwi body smell come from? At the time of writing, I am studying the seasonal composition of odorous chemicals in faeces and in the preen gland secretion. This last one is especially interesting because a kiwi rubs the secretion all over its body. Faeces, like other body secretions, may contain chemical information such as breeding status, sex and perhaps age. All of this information is like a type of ID card.

Figure 4: Sniffing behaviour of kiwi.

When a kiwi 'sniffs', air is inhaled noisily through the nostrils. As a prelude to this act, a bird in the open often stretches its body vertically and lifts its bill into the air in exaggerated fashion, causing the neck to bend and the head to be drawn backwards. The bird then moves the bill in small arches. Drawings at either end show kiwi in alert (far left) and normal foraging postures (far right) with the head held below the level of the back. Disturbed kiwi often freeze in position (in this case mid-step) before displaying olfactory behaviour.

WHAT DO KIWI SMELL LIKE?

Describing any kind of smell is highly subjective, but I will try to tell you how kiwi smell. As mentioned on page 31, the faeces smell quite unlike the bird itself. (In fact, they smell very different from the droppings of other birds, such as chickens.) The faeces smell resembles a blend of ammonia and terpene, and you can get a hint of this by taking a tawa fruit in your hands and rubbing it until the juices are released. The smell is strong and easy to detect even when you are walking in the bush; I have found several kiwi burrows simply by following my nose! And I think this is the way dogs, in many cases, find them too. The smell of the bird, on the other hand, is more like that of a cat or dog: a rather sweet

Kiwi faeces smell strongly. Scientists are trying to find out if kiwi can communicate using these smells.

and musky odour, with a hint of moss that derives, perhaps, from being in the bush. In our study site, brown kiwi often smell like faeces. Brown kiwi deposit faeces inside, at the entrance or on the way to the burrow. The birds seem to rub faeces on themselves when they move in, out and around the burrow. It is unknown if this is done purposefully, but if it is this would provide information to other kiwi.

The Department of Conservation has a small number of specially trained dogs which help find kiwi by following their strong scent back to their burrows.

Hearing

The importance of hearing in kiwi is signalled loud and clear by the sheer size of the external earholes, which can be seen behind the eyes: they're enormous! The area of the kiwi brain involved with processing auditory information is correspondingly well developed. This is hardly surprising for a nocturnal bird that uses the forest floor. Kiwi seem to hear best at frequencies within the range of 500 to 5000 Hz. In comparison, human hearing is keenest at frequencies between 20 and 20,000 Hz. Kiwi therefore have a narrower hearing range than we do, and in particular cannot hear high-pitched sounds. A number of features in the brain and ear seem to indicate, however, that they can hear best the higher frequencies within their auditory range, a characteristic that kiwi share with barn owls. Interestingly, the rustling sound made on leaf litter by insects and other animals falls within this high-frequency range. Barn owls appear to rely on such sounds to track their prey, and it has been suggested that kiwi do likewise when foraging.

Recent observations of wild kiwi during their active periods at night revealed that birds spent most of their time foraging, and that they did

Large exposed ear openings behind the eye indicate the importance of hearing to kiwi. Long 'whiskers' and a sensitive tip to the end of the beak provide a delicate sense of touch, which allows kiwi to function in total darkness.

Often a kiwi's first response to a strange sound, smell or movement in the distance is simply to 'freeze' and listen while remaining silent. Such behaviour was no defence against a fast-moving vehicle for this female great spotted kiwi killed on the Arthur's Pass road.

so mostly by probing in the leaf litter and into the soil. Kiwi rarely caught prey that was moving on the surface. Observers were too far away from the birds to hear the rustling of small invertebrates moving in leaf litter, nor could they detect any behaviour – such as cocking the head – which might have indicated the kiwi were actively listening for prey. (Experiments with captive kiwi showed that hearing was not involved in prey detection of buried prey, either.) However, the observers could hear louder rustling sounds made by larger animals stepping on the forest litter at night – such as other kiwi, or rats. Kiwi responded to these louder sounds by raising the head and orienting it in the direction from which the sound came. Kiwi were also very sensitive to people and other birds making noise when walking or moving on the leaf litter. So it is possible that this sensitivity toward rustling sounds helps kiwi remain alert to predators or other kiwi and to gain awareness of their surroundings.

Vocalisations

It seems reasonable to suppose that a nocturnal species relies heavily on calling to communicate with others of its kind. Kiwi make a number of calls, the best-known of which is the 'whistle call' of a male, a cry that rings loud and clear in the forest night. Interestingly, across all of the species male and female kiwi produce different whistle calls, so that a listener can easily distinguish the sexes. Both male and female calls consist of a

In close proximity a courting pair of rowi, or Okarito brown kiwi, make soft grunting, growling and squeaky sounds as they cautiously circle each other.

repetitive series of notes, but while the males' are clear whistles, females produce more guttural, grunty notes. As in most kiwi research, work on vocalisations has mostly been done on brown kiwi. In this species (and we can expect to find the same in all species), the differences between male and female calls are reflected in their frequency: while female calls range between 0.1 and 7 kHz, male calls have a broader range of 1.5 to 13 kHz. The upshot of this is that the higher-pitched male calls carry further than female calls and, as it happens, are more audible to the human ear.

The song of female brown kiwi was found to contain *formants*. Formants, an important feature of language, are caused by the modulation of sound by structures such as the tongue and lips. In humans formants allow the identification of letters and thus words, and in other species they have been found to communicate important information such as body size and individual identity. A further interesting aspect of brown kiwi calls is that there is a great deal of variation among individual birds, and it has been suggested that individuals may be identifiable by their call. The vocalisations of little spotted kiwi are quite unlike those of any other kiwi species; the female's song in particular is less guttural, being more of a trilling sound.

Although no systematic age/vocalisation studies have yet been done, kiwi have been heard first calling at six months old. As for most young birds of other species, they probably do not call regularly until they reach adulthood. Once they do, however, calling becomes an important part of the routine. Kiwi begin calling on the first hour of darkness and continue to call throughout the night. It appears that males call more than females. Sometimes, duets are heard. This occurs when members of a pair or a group call simultaneously; in brown kiwi, for instance, females duet by responding to male calls.

The high occurrence of calls, along with the fact that male and female calls differ, has enabled researchers to develop a monitoring tool called *call surveying*, which they use to chart the status of kiwi populations. Listening stations are located at high points in areas where kiwi live, and recordings are made for the first two hours of darkness over four or five days in a row; the sex of the calls and their direction (using a compass) are also logged. From these data managers calculate a call rate per hour, which can be used to detect increases or decreases in population size.

Our knowledge of kiwi vocal communication is still in its infancy. We still do not really know why kiwi call. Is it to maintain their territory? To cement pair bonds? Or both? Or does it enable them to work out where other neighbouring kiwi are and to detect important foraging areas, or to meet up with others? Much work remains to be done. For instance, kiwi are known to respond to pre-recorded broadcasts of calls, so scientists are planning to conduct experiments in which they record specific kiwi calls and then play them back to birds of different sex or age or location, and observe their reactions – to find out, as it were, what a call 'means' to a kiwi.

A North Island brown kiwi foraging at night.

FOOD AND FORAGING

The kiwi diet

It is hard to identify what kiwi eat by direct observation alone: this is partly because of their nocturnal habits and their technique of probing for hidden prey, and also because they can be very quick to swallow anything captured! Accordingly, when studying the kiwi diet scientists use a couple of alternative strategies. They most often examine the faeces of live birds and pick out the small undigested bits and pieces from animals and plants consumed. They can also analyse food remains from the gizzard contents of dead birds. To identify which animals and plants these remains come from, researchers make what they call 'identification keys'. They catch invertebrate prey and collect fruits and plants from the study areas and preserve them in an agent such as ethanol. Items from the faeces or stomach contents can then be compared with these preserved 'keys'. Collecting the available foods within kiwi habitat is also a good way of finding out whether the birds simply eat what's there or whether they have some preferred food sources that are actively sought, even when scarce.

Because invertebrate life cycles vary seasonally and between species, collections need to be done regularly through the year, for example at monthly or bimonthly intervals. This is not as easy as it may seem, particularly if researchers want to learn about the relative abundance of invertebrate species. Collection techniques include the use of pitfall traps: ground-level containers into which invertebrates fall as they move about. (While this type of sampling gathers a wide variety of species, some nocturnal, others diurnal, it does not sample flying insects.) A small amount of ethanol or some such agent is placed in each container to both subdue and preserve the trapped samples. Every two to four weeks, traps are emptied, and then begins the even harder job of identification. A more appropriate sampling method would be to remove the top 10 cm layer of soil and search through it for invertebrates. This is difficult, however, and not only because the soil can be hard to dig. Owing to the typically 'clustered' distribution of invertebrates over an area of soil, we would have to dig a great deal in order to obtain a true idea of what is available. And here is another potential worry: are our methods of collecting and analysing the kiwi's diet significantly depleting its food resources?

Collecting kiwi faeces in the wild involves walking through an area where kiwi are known to live and finding them on the ground; their strong smell (see page 32) and large size can make location relatively

Earthworms comprise 40–45 per cent of a kiwi's diet, although it is normally difficult to observe a kiwi – such as this female great spotted kiwi – actively consuming them.

easy. Brown kiwi sometimes defecate in or near the entrance of their burrows, and so collection at these sites is also possible. Researchers take care, however, not to disturb birds while resting; this may involve tracking radio transmitter-carrying birds to their shelters, and then waiting until nightfall (when the birds leave to feed) before collecting faeces.

So what *do* kiwi eat? Even with faeces to study, it is hard to say categorically. Most research to date has been on the brown kiwi diet, with a single study each on the little spotted kiwi and Stewart Island tokoeka. The results show differences in the diet that may be explained by location and time of the year of the field study, or the species of kiwi studied. For these reasons more research is required for a clearer picture of kiwi diet and to establish whether each species has a particular diet or even if different foods are required at different times of the year. But if we assume that the results are representative of all kiwi, we can say that adult kiwi eat a mostly carnivorous diet plus a few fruits.

Earthworms are the main component of the diet (40–45 per cent), with other invertebrates, including insects, forming a similar proportion (40–45 per cent) and plant material, especially fruits, completing the mix.

A female Stewart Island tokoeka forages above the tide for sand-hoppers hiding beneath the kelp.

Of the insect prey, underground larvae and nymphs of relatively large insects, such as cicadas and beetles, are consumed. The diet of chicks has been studied on only three occasions, all of them relating to brown kiwi, but it seems to include insect larvae (including caterpillars), adult beetles, weta, centipedes, millipedes and earthworms. The kiwi diet on the whole appears to follow the local availability of invertebrates. That said, the sheer numbers of some larvae (including crane fly and scarabid beetles) in faeces, compared with their availability in the soil, suggest that kiwi actively seek these foods.

Within days of hatching out of the egg, young North Island brown kiwi are actively foraging for food in the forest litter.

THE CAPTIVE DIET

A few kiwi are kept in captivity for display purposes in zoos and nocturnal houses in New Zealand and around the world. Young kiwi are also kept captive for a few weeks or months as part of Operation Nest Egg (see page 67). Some kiwi in captivity breed successfully, others do not. Also, a number of captive kiwi suffer from obesity. The problem seems to be associated with diet (and lack of exercise), and for this reason there has been a great deal of interest in revising the diet offered to birds in captivity, matching it more closely to what kiwi eat in the wild. A team at Massey University has developed a diet in a series of steps.

First, the researchers calculated the protein, fat, carbohydrates and mineral/vitamin content of wild birds' diet from the stomach contents of dead birds. Next, they reconstructed the diet based on the content of these molecules in wild foods. (They calculated, for example, how many beetles, earthworms and rimu fruits were needed to produce a diet offering x per cent of protein, y carbohydrates, and z fats). And, finally, they developed an *artificial* diet, using more common foods such as meat, fruits and vege-tables, which resembled as closely as possible the reconstructed diet. This diet has been trialled on kiwi … and they seem to like it!

The kiwi captive diet may include sliced oxheart, tofu, cereals and vitamin additives. The new diet aims to match as closely as possible to the protein/ fat/carbohydrate levels in a wild kiwi's diet.

Diet and competition

The greatest concern of kiwi conservationists has always been the impact of introduced mammals as predators. Recently, however, there is an increasing interest in the effect of mammals as rivals for vital resources. It is well known that when two species share a similar ecological niche there will be competition for shared resources. Kiwi are principally carnivorous, feeding on a variety of invertebrates. Rats, mice and hedgehogs have a similar diet and could be important competitors. In 1999, for instance, Christopher Berry, a Masters student of Conservation Science at Victoria University of Wellington, presented a report to the Department of Conservation on how kiwi might be facing competition from hedgehogs in the Boundary Stream Mainland Island reserve in Hawke's Bay. He calculated that the hedgehog population in this area, which he put at around 4500 individuals, could be removing a staggering 660 kg of invertebrates from the reserve each night. Clearly kiwi, with their similar diet, could be affected. Rats, too, have been proved extremely harmful. (My team's research into the effect of high densities of rats, cats, kiwi and morepork upon invertebrate life has shown that rats have the greatest impact on invertebrate density.) When Norway rats and kiore (Polynesian rats) were eradicated from Kapiti Island, kiwi density increased, suggesting that these rodents had been competing with kiwi for resources.

Hedgehogs, introduced nocturnal insectivores that have a similar diet to our native kiwi, may be competing with kiwi for the same food resources.

Haast tokoeka habitat in South Westland.

A KIWI HABITAT

Habitat use and territoriality

The only detailed published studies of habitat use and territoriality are on brown kiwi (in Hawke's Bay, Paerata and Waitangi and on Ponui Island), so there is still much to be learnt about the other species. And as is the case with so much kiwi research, these studies have used small samples of individual kiwi at different locations, so the results should be regarded with caution because they may not be representative of all brown kiwi.

Kiwi are found in all habitat types, including native mature forest, regenerating scrub, exotic plantations, swamps and farm pasture, from sea level to the alpine zone. Researchers Michael and Barbara Taborski, studying a population in Waitangi Forest, found a favourite habitat, regardless of activity, to be seral vegetation. ('Seral' describes plant communities that are in intermediate stages of succession. In New Zealand we often talk about seral vegetation when it includes introduced species interspersed with natives.) Other kiwi habitats included native bush, pine forest, and road/pasture areas for foraging; marshland for roosting; and native bush for nesting. In two studies at Trounson Kauri Park, Northland, kiwi chicks and juveniles preferred seral vegetation to mature forest. Young chicks spent the first few weeks using habitats close to their nest, but as they grew older they went much further afield into

In many areas in the North Island, seral vegetation (vegetation in intermediate stages of succession) is an important habitat for kiwi.

seral vegetation and/or pasture depending on the season. Interestingly, chicks or juveniles that used several habitat types instead of just one grew at a faster pace and lived longer. Both studies found that adults and chicks used different habitats, and the authors have suggested that this behavioural difference could be an evolutionary adaptation that helps eliminate direct competition between the two age classes.

It seems that some brown kiwi populations are territorial and others are not. (Animals are said to be territorial when individuals – or pairs – occupy a particular area to the exclusion of other individuals or pairs. The term 'home range' is used for an area that is occupied, but not necessarily defended.) Four pairs in Hawke's Bay used a total area of 770 ha (representing a low density of one bird per 55 ha) and had territories that did not overlap at all. By contrast, two high-density populations at Paerata (where 23 birds were studied) and Waitangi (51 birds) differed greatly in their organisation. At Waitangi, with a density of 18.5 birds per ha, kiwi were territorial and there was little overlap between pairs' territories, while in Paerata (2.5 kiwi per ha) neighbouring home ranges overlapped fully and there was no territoriality at all. Kiwi on Ponui Island (10 kiwi per ha) also had overlapping home ranges and were not territorial. In all of these populations, despite the best efforts of researchers, few direct physical interactions between kiwi have been seen. It has been suggested that kiwi maintain their territory by calling and perhaps by using scent posts; for example, kiwi have defecated in burrows that were later used by other individuals, suggesting that these excreta may act as a message. In our study population on Ponui Island kiwi are known to 'go walkabout' away from their home range areas into neighbouring home ranges, sometimes for days.

Underground living

When birds are inactive or sleeping they are also said to be *roosting* and the place of rest is known as a *roost*. Kiwi use a variety of shelters for roosting as well as for nesting. In our study site, they mostly use underground burrows, which can be excavated by kiwi themselves or formed when trees fall. The roots of large trees, particularly those close to the trunk, may be thick, and when uprooted they leave holes – sometimes several in one location. Our group refers to multiple root cavities as kiwi *apartment buildings* and often we may find birds inside several of the holes. Kiwi also like to roost in hollow trees, both those that have fallen down and those that are standing but have entrances at the base. Kiwi aren't too fussy:

A well-camouflaged North Island brown kiwi sleeping out in the open at the base of a pohutukawa tree. Notice the white faeces at the base of the leaning branch.

Duncan, a kiwi manager for DOC, returning a rowi, or Okarito brown kiwi, to its burrow after a radio transmitter attachment.

more than once, I have found birds a metre or two above ground inside leaning hollow trees. Kiwi also like to roost inside holes created by the water in dry banks and beds of streams, and also cavities in and among rocks. Many times, kiwi choose less substantial roosting sites, such as a clump of kahakaha (*Collospermum*), *Astelia* or similar thick vegetation. In swamps they roost in cavities formed by clumps of vegetation. They

A female great spotted kiwi in her nesting burrow. Notice the large amount of accumulated nesting material.

Mark, a kiwi manager for DOC, extracts a brown kiwi from its burrow deep within a tangle of roots beneath a fallen tree in the Maungatautari Ecological Island Reserve.

will even roost under just one or two leaves, or place their heads against a small bankside depression and go to sleep. Burrows may have single entrances, but sometimes they have more than one.

Why are kiwi burrows so interesting? For a start, the kiwi seems to be the only bird that uses burrows year round, not just for nesting, for example. Also, the kiwi's use of burrows help us find out about kiwi social life, because kiwi have been found to share favourite roosts with other kiwi that they have close associations with. When birds in our study group 'tire' of one roost, they may move to another, and then other birds may use the abandoned site. Not surprisingly, this behaviour is very common during the breeding season when birds are most likely to be looking for mates.

Recently hatched North Island brown kiwi.

BREEDING KIWI

The Department of Conservation has been recording for many years now the breeding output of all species of kiwi as part of Operation Nest Egg (ONE) (see page 67). The problem with information collected for ONE is that eggs are removed from the parents before they hatch, and so the production of eggs and chicks is not exactly as it would be if the birds were left to their own devices. For this reason, the information below is sourced solely from published accounts of kiwi breeding behaviour and success; to date, there are just three, and all are on brown kiwi.

Courtship and mating

What little we know about mating in wild kiwi comes only from brief encounters with the birds at night and survives in the memories of the lucky observers. Here I describe what my student Susan Cunningham was lucky enough to film once during her studies. It was the breeding season of 2007/08 and she was recording kiwi foraging behaviour using a handheld infrared video camera when she heard a short repetitive grunt. My students and I had been wondering as to the meaning of this grunt; it is a familiar sound during the breeding season, so we had suspected it meant something special. Susie's film would prove this to be so. She was in a typical New Zealand paddock of short grass and a sprinkling of sedges that offered excellent visibility. She filmed two kiwi, a male walking rapidly after a female, and it was hard to tell which of the two was grunting. It looked as though he was chasing her, but they did not travel far and stayed within filming range. After an hour, they stopped, and the male made a short call to which the female responded with another short call. She then crouched on the grass; he touched her back with his bill and climbed on top of her to mate. Unlike mammals, birds do not have external copulatory organs and the intestinal, genital and urinary tracts all finish in a single large area known as the cloaca. To copulate, birds need to place their cloacae in contact in order for sperm to be transferred from the male to the female. Kiwi males, like the males of all other palaeognaths, ducks, geese and swans, have something resembling a penis, which holds onto the female during copulation. Perched on the female's back, the male (looking rather like a brown ball) appeared to have flipped himself backwards perhaps to achieve cloacal contact, or perhaps he had lost control and fell over. And that was it. The birds then resumed their grunting 'chase', this time away from Susie's camera and heading into the night.

A pair of North Island brown kiwi together in a nesting burrow.

MATING SYSTEMS IN BIRDS

The way in which each bird species goes about mating seems to be governed by environmental conditions (such as the seasonal availability of food resources), and the evolutionary history of that species (or, as one might put it, the history of its relationship to other species). Let us imagine, for example, a species in which a female requires x amount of food to successfully produce offspring. Let's assume, too, that its environment contains food in small 'clumps', each of more than Ix. A male that can occupy an area containing 3x, and defend it against competitors, might therefore attract and mate with three females, all of which could successfully produce his offspring. Such a mating system, where a male mates with more than one female, is called *polygyny*. Now let us take an environment in which food resources are thinly spread and a male is able only to defend an area containing Ix; he can have only one female, and the mating system would be monogamous. These examples are an oversimplification of the facts, but they help to illustrate scientific thinking. Other basic mating systems include polyandry (when a female mates with more than one male) and polygynandry (when many males and many females mate with one another). Polygamy is another acceptable term for the various mating systems, such as polyandry, polygyny and polygynandry, that involve matings between more than one male and one female.

When all the individuals in these mating systems help with territorial defence or egg and chick care, we say they are engaging in communal breeding, or that they have a cooperative mating system. But while it is romantic to think that animals cooperate altruistically with one another, we have to ask: why would an individual forfeit or reduce its *own* reproduction to live in a group and help others with

Pukeko are an example of a polygynandrous mating system, where a group composed of several males and several females all participate in mating.

their reproduction? Well, for some species of birds, brothers and/or sisters from previous years stay in the parents' territories and help them by taking over some breeding duties. In some cases they do this because the resources available in the environment are not enough to allow each individual to breed as part of a pair, and much help is necessary to raise a single young. In these cases, the helping birds are indirectly passing on their genes by ensuring their siblings survive. In some species, helpers gain valuable parenting practice that makes them more successful breeders when conditions allow them to breed for themselves. In other species, however, members of groups are not genetically related. Through modern DNA fingerprinting we can now establish that in many cases helpers actually gain some paternity or maternity – in other words, they are mating successfully. So much for altruism!

Before the advent of genetic parentage techniques, it was believed that 90 per cent of bird species were monogamous. Today we know that most of the species studied, while apparently monogamous, produce offspring that does not belong to the male at the nest. In fact, in Australasia, many bird species display cooperative breeding, including some kiwi species.

Multiple breeding systems

Kiwi breeding and parenting systems vary with species, but overall a high degree of flexibility seems to be the pattern, with mating strategies ranging from monogamy to cooperative breeding. Even when a male and a female are breeding as a pair, DNA analysis shows that the resulting chick may not be the offspring of the male. For instance, most Fiordland and Haast tokoeka, rowi and great spotted kiwi breed in pairs, while most Stewart Island tokoeka breed in family groups. Rowi may also be able to breed in family groups, although low population densities and high youngster mortality make it difficult to establish this. Until recently, little spotted kiwi and brown kiwi were said to breed in pairs, but it now seems that brown kiwi are more flexible than this. Brown kiwi on Ponui Island have been known to breed in groups of adult birds, mostly two males and one female, but sometimes groups are larger.

Another unusual characteristic of kiwi is that two of the species, the

little spotted and brown kiwi, exhibit what is called sex role reversal, in that the male takes over incubation, which is more usually a female job. Both parents incubate eggs in Fiordland and Haast tokoeka, rowi and great spotted kiwi, while several members of a Stewart Island tokoeka family seem to incubate. There is also some flexibility in this, however. For example, a brown kiwi female has been recorded incubating eggs in Northland and other females have been found inside nests during the incubation period, although it was unclear whether they were incubating; little spotted kiwi females were found sharing incubation with males; and in our study site when

Although little spotted kiwi breed in pairs, it is the male, and not the female, who takes over the role of incubating the egg.

Male and female North Island brown kiwi in the nest together. It will be the male, rather than the female, who will take over the role of incubating the egg after it is laid.

breeding in groups all the males within a group share the nest (sometimes simultaneously, at other times sequentially) and may be incubating. Members of the extended kiwi family, the palaeognaths and tinamous, express a variety of mating systems, so it is not surprising that kiwi do the same.

We are unsure why kiwi breed like this. Generally, it seems that cooperative breeding becomes more common towards the south of the country. Perhaps both parents (and other family members, too) help with incubation in the south because of the colder temperatures. Or perhaps different predation pressures in the South Island during the kiwi's evolutionary history made it safer to have a parent guarding the egg all of the time. What's certain is that more study is required.

Incubation

Incubation involves the production of heat by a parent bird and the transfer of heat to the eggs so that the embryos can grow. In most birds, including kiwi, heat is transferred from a brood patch, an abdominal area lacking in feathers where the exposed skin is warmed by blood vessels. The temperature needs to be kept within a range of 37–38 °C; anything higher or lower and the embryos may die. The parent must also turn the eggs to ensure they are warmed throughout. Clearly, the parent bird has to leave the nest periodically (to feed, for instance, or preen), at which

An adult brown kiwi leaving its well-camouflaged nest at dusk. Unlike roosting burrows which often have large obvious entrances, nest entrances are usually small and well covered with any available surrounding material.

Left: Some North Island brown kiwi partially bury their eggs in the nesting material – the reason for this behaviour is still unknown.

Below: The first sign of 'pipping' is when the kiwi chick inside the egg first cracks the shell.

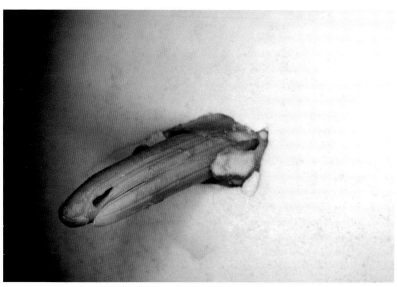

The hatching chick's bill, protruding from the shell, ensures an adequate supply of oxygen prior to finally breaking out of the shell. The slit towards the end of the bill is the kiwi's nostril.

point the eggs gradually cool and development of the embryo is slowed; the longer the parent is away, the colder the eggs get and the more energy the parent must expend to rewarm them. In cold weather or an exposed location, eggs will cool faster. Humidity is also very important for embryos to develop properly. Because the shell is permeable, eggs lose water when they are warmed; if they lose too much, they may never hatch.

Winter breeding

Generally, all kiwi species breed over the winter and spring months. This may sound odd, since most animals breed during the spring and summer, and breeding in winter, as mentioned above, may make it harder to keep eggs warm. Scientists suspect kiwi nest in the winter because of the longer nights, which allow these nocturnal birds more time for socialising and foraging, two activities that assist in successful breeding. Kiwi are believed to cope by nesting underground, mostly within excavated burrows, where eggs may be kept relatively warm while the parent is away. It is possible also that the nesting burrow allows the bird some control over humidity. Sometimes male brown kiwi and little spotted kiwi cover the entrance of the nest with vegetation when they leave, and while this may be done to camouflage the nest itself, it could also help maintain humidity. Rowi, which live in a more humid environment, do not display this behaviour, while Stewart Island tokoeka sometimes cover the entrance (even with the other incubating bird inside). Kiwi also use vegetation to line the nest and probably keep the eggs warm while the incubating parent is away. Interestingly, brown kiwi and great spotted kiwi seem to have different incubation behaviours. Brown kiwi eggs are often found buried in vegetation to the point that they may be invisible to someone looking into the burrow. The male squats on the eggs to incubate them. In contrast, the eggs of the great spotted kiwi are placed over matted vegetation and are therefore exposed (although because both parents incubate, the eggs are never left in the open). Instead of squatting on eggs, great spotted kiwi parents cradle them on their toes, providing heat all round. The reasons for these differences in behaviour are unclear, but may be down to climate or the threat of a predator, or even the size of the egg.

Big egg, advanced chick, brief care

Some kiwi species lay a single clutch of one egg per year, while others lay two clutches and up to two eggs per clutch (for more details, see the section on species accounts, pages 76–85). Weighing 300 g or more, depending on the species, kiwi eggs are incredibly large. In terms of egg size relative to female body size, they are exceeded only by the eggs of the megapodes of Australia and southeastern Asia. Kiwi eggs are, nonetheless, the richest eggs described so far in terms of energy content, averaging some 4014 kJ (959 kcal) per egg. A typical 16-year-old girl, measuring 1.6 m in height and weighing 54 kg, has energy requirements of about 9500 kJ per day. This is equivalent to the energy in 2.5 kiwi eggs – or 28 chicken eggs! Kiwi eggs also have a disproportionately large egg yolk, constituting about 65 per cent of the total egg volume. The growing chick utilises most of the yolk while in the egg, but it hatches with enough yolk in its belly to last for five to 10 days after hatching. In fact, the belly

A domestic hen's egg alongside the much larger egg of a North Island brown kiwi.

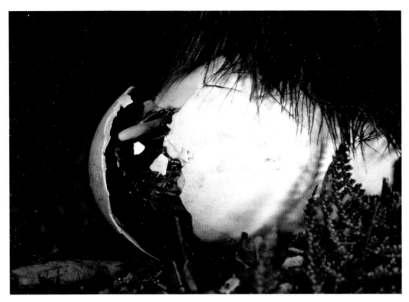

Hatching can be a prolonged and tiring process for a kiwi chick. After heaving and flexing inside the shell, the chick creates a wide crack around one end. As the integrity of the shell slowly weakens, other cracks begin to appear across the shell. The chick flexes more actively now, using its feet to kick the collapsing shell apart.

Once free of the shell, the chick rests. In the warmth of the burrow its feathers slowly dry and it begins to look more like a tiny replica of its parents.

of a newly hatched kiwi chick feels very squashy because of the large amount of yolk it contains.

The kiwi also holds a near-record in terms of length of incubation, which lasts for 65–85 days (depending on the species), a duration surpassed only by some species of albatross (which also lay large eggs). The huge rich egg, together with the long incubation period, produces a chick that is quite independent at hatching. In fact, it looks like a small version of its parents, with a full set of adult-looking feathers, and it is not fed by its parents nor is it accompanied by them when it leaves the nest to forage. Brown kiwi chicks spend only six to 25 days with their father before leaving home for good. Given that the chick is so independent, why spend any time at all with its parent? Perhaps it helps keep the chick warm for as long as possible with the least necessary expenditure of energy.

Duncan Kaye, a kiwi manager for DOC, with a rowi, or Okarito brown kiwi.

CONSERVATION

Chicks under pressure

Unfortunately, each species of kiwi today is threatened or in danger of extinction. Populations of all species have declined throughout their range and in some places become extinct. I believe there are two main reasons why we still have *any* kiwi at all; the first is that kiwi are long-lived, and the second is that the various forest-dwelling mammalian predators that have been introduced into New Zealand are small. The main reason why kiwi are endangered is that there is no recruitment of chicks into the adult population. There are plenty of old birds, but no younger generations to replace them because one introduced predator in particular, the stoat, kills young kiwi. It is lucky that we realised what was happening before most adults died of old age, and that we still have breeding birds. Let us briefly picture the scenario if, instead of mustelids (stoats, weasels and ferrets) to control rabbits, the early settlers had introduced the much larger fox, as happened in Australia. Foxes would have most likely eaten the adult birds, and with the adults gone, the various kiwi species would probably have died out a long time ago. As an example, the little spotted kiwi – the smallest species, whose adults can be killed by stoats and ferrets – became extinct on the mainland very rapidly after the introduction of mustelids to New Zealand in the late nineteenth century.

How come kiwi are so vulnerable to introduced predators such as the mustelids? It is because they have adapted to live in a world that, until recently, contained no stoat-like predators. Today's kiwi are the product of a long process of natural selection in which their ancestors evolved to live a nocturnal life foraging for invertebrates underground or on the surface litter, with many other animals competing for the same food sources, and mostly other birds for predators. Indeed, predators are a major selective pressure upon the appearance and behaviour of an animal. In the case of kiwi, the list of possible predators includes two known nocturnal species: the laughing owl, which is known to have taken little spotted kiwi and probably also chicks of other kiwi species; and the tuatara, an ancient reptile that, although slow-moving, may have been able to catch kiwi chicks. Adzebills, which were large, rail-like predatory birds, became extinct around AD 1400. It is not known whether they were active by day or at night, but they may have been able to take prey weighing up to 2 kg, which would include little spotted kiwi, chicks from all kiwi species, and even some kiwi males of any of the brown varieties. The Australasian harrier, although diurnal, spends much time in swamps, which are known to be good habitat for kiwi, so it may take

Tuatara once occurred on mainland New Zealand, and would have hunted similar food to kiwi (in this case a tree weta). Indeed tuatara may well have been predators of young kiwi themselves.

Australasian harriers may hunt and kill young kiwi foraging during the day in wetlands or other marginal areas.

the odd chick as well. The extinct Haast's eagle and Forbes' harrier, both diurnal birds, may also have taken kiwi chicks and adults. I believe certain kiwi behaviours evolved as defence against predators such as these. For example, kiwi freeze when surprised at a surface roost, and when scared they run and hide (for example by entering a burrow or hiding the head against vegetation). These behaviours may fool a hunting bird, especially when these are larger than the kiwi, looking for prey from above and at a distance, or a slow-moving tuatara, but they do not discourage a small, sinuous hunter like a stoat.

An adult tokoeka, killed by a dog near Oban, Stewart Island. Uncontrolled dogs kill kiwi. Simple measures such as kennelling dogs before dark significantly reduce kiwi mortality.

Back in 1891, the well-known New Zealand naturalist Walter Buller voiced his concerns regarding the fate of kiwi and other flightless native birds, such as kakapo, in the presence of introduced mustelids, which had recently been released into the wild in an effort to control rabbits. Predicting that if nothing was done these species would become extinct, he advocated for birds to be translocated to islands where there were no predators. It is estimated that during the century which followed Buller's prediction, kiwi populations declined by 90 per cent. By the early 1990s, former densities of 40 to 100 adult kiwi per hectare in New Zealand forests were down to about four kiwi per hectare. (Some sites – islands such as Kapiti, and some areas in Northland – still have high densities of 50 to 100 kiwi per hectare, but this is rare.)

The truth about predators

It was a research paper in 1996 that finally proved predators, more than any other factor, have been causing the decline of kiwi populations. This seminal work put together by John McLennan (but carried out by a number of people all over New Zealand) showed that, in general, adult brown kiwi and great spotted kiwi can defend themselves against most predators, but that if the predators were eliminated, kiwi would live longer and increase their reproductive output by as much as 60 per cent. For example, adults would live 18.7 years on average in contrast to 11.7 and potentially produce up to 28 extra eggs (four per year) in the seven extra years of life. Dogs and ferrets particularly, but also pigs and possums, were found to be able to kill adult kiwi. This study found that eggs did not seem to suffer much predation by mammals (a 10 per cent loss), although many eggs (up to 60 per cent) did not hatch. (The reason for the hatching failures may be bacteria growing in the eggs, but more studies are needed.) The most shocking finding was that of the 49 brown kiwi chicks studied only an estimated two to nine (5–18 per cent) reached adulthood. Of the young birds killed by predators, mammals killed at least 8 per cent of chicks and 45 per cent of juveniles. Mustelids (mostly stoats, but also weasels) were responsible for 77 per cent of deaths while two chicks (15.4 per cent) were killed by cats. A single chick (7.6 per cent) was killed by an avian predator, a harrier. Data modelling showed that it would take 65 years to reduce a kiwi population from 100 to two kiwi per hectare if the average loss rate is 5.8 per cent. Mortality of young would need to be reduced by at least 34 per cent of current levels to stop kiwi populations declining.

The research by McLennan and collaborators was extremely important because it demonstrated with facts and figures what had up until then seemed scarcely believable. It thus played a crucial part in getting enough funding to protect kiwi, and also it showed that other species in New Zealand forests may be suffering from mammalian predation. Based on this new information, two main conservation strategies were implemented: Operation Nest Egg and kiwi sanctuaries (zones).

Stoats, introduced into New Zealand by humans in order to control rabbits, are now the major cause of mortality in young kiwi and are thus responsible for the kiwi's endangered status across New Zealand.

This great spotted kiwi chick is the same age as the dead chick above, but thanks to Operation Nest Egg its chances of survival are greatly enhanced through human intervention.

ISLAND SANCTUARIES AND TRANSLOCATION

In 1891, the year of Buller's bleak prediction, Resolution Island was gazetted as a sanctuary for native wildlife. New Zealand's fifth-largest island, Resolution lies off the western tip of Fiordland, isolated by Dusky and Breaksea sounds, and its name is closely tied to that of Richard Henry. Originally from Ireland but raised in Australia, Henry came to New Zealand as a young man and became an outdoorsman and a writer.

Appointed curator/caretaker of Resolution in 1894, he began to translocate kiwi, weka and kakapo to the island in the hope they would survive there. Unfortunately, Resolution was close enough to the mainland for stoats to swim across the sounds in around 1900, and all the translocated birds there died. Henry, who later curated the wildlife on Kapiti Island, is remembered today as New Zealand's first conservation officer.

Richard Henry safely translocated kakapo (left) and weka (below) to islands.

Despite the failure of Henry's efforts on Resolution, translocations have become one of the major tools used by conservation managers to preserve the species we still have. In the case of kiwi, the programme has had its ups and downs through time. Translocations of kiwi initiated in Henry's time by the Department of Lands and Survey continued until about 1915, after which the programme lost momentum as it became clear that native species were losing the battle against introduced predators. However, island releases have continued at a much slower pace (but more successfully) to the present day, thanks to improvements in the methods we use to eradicate introduced mammals. Island translocations are the only reason why we still have little spotted kiwi, the smallest and most vulnerable of kiwi species. Islands are also used as crèches to allow kiwi chicks of all kiwi species to grow wild and safe until reaching a weight that will allow them to survive in the presence of mammalian predators.

Islands have served, too, as inspiration for the development of *mainland islands*: these are areas in mainland New Zealand that have been isolated from the rest of the land around them either by means of a predator-proof fence or by the continuous control of predators within a core area.

The forests of Stewart Island, or Rakiura, support healthy populations of Stewart Island tokoeka, and are still one of the best places to encounter kiwi in the wild.

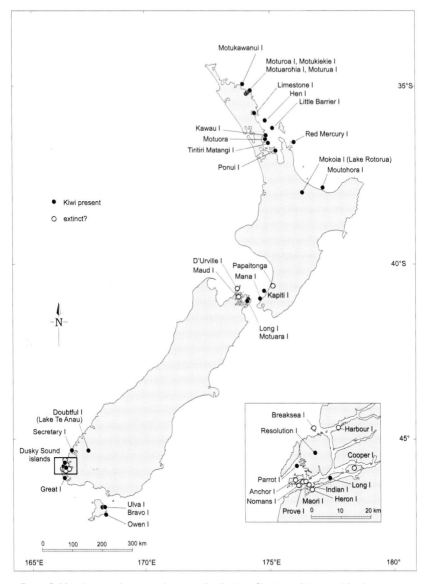

Figure 5: Map showing the past and present distribution of kiwi populations on islands.

Source: Rogan Colbourne/DOC.

Operation Nest Egg

Operation Nest Egg (ONE) is a programme developed to help kiwi survive into adulthood. Launched in 1994, it has been extremely successful. At its heart is a simple, but brilliant, idea: to take into captivity those stages of the kiwi life cycle that are least successful in the wild, improve on them where possible, and then return their products to the wild. It had been clear from the studies to date that a large proportion of kiwi eggs were not hatching, and that most kiwi chicks were not surviving to adulthood because they were being eaten by mustelids. Researchers knew that if they could only improve the survival rate of eggs and chicks and boost their recruitment into adulthood, and thus increase the breeding population, kiwi could be taken off the endangered list.

The programme has three stages: collecting wild eggs, incubating and hatching them in captivity, and rearing chicks in a predator-free environment until they reach a size where they are capable of fending off mammalian predators and can be re-released into their wild habitat. Sometimes, recently hatched chicks found in wild nests have also been taken in, reared to the appropriate size and then re-released. Though it is not easy to return an animal to the wild after a period in captivity, some

Wild rowi eggs from Okarito Forest are collected and transported to ONE facilities for hatching and chick rearing to a predator-safe size, before being returned to the sanctuary.

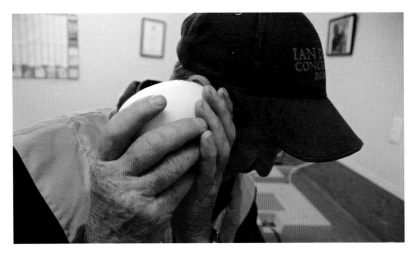

A few days prior to hatching, kiwi chicks begin to call inside the egg. The tiny sound can be heard if you hold the egg close to your ear.

of the kiwi's natural characteristics help make such a project possible. As already explained, newly hatched kiwi chicks are highly developed compared with other birds' chicks, and become completely independent from their parents just a few weeks after hatching. All they are thought to receive from their parents and/or carers after hatching is bodily warmth. These chicks never need to be fed or shown how to feed by their parents to survive. Also, people have been incubating eggs of other bird species and hatching them in captivity for a long time now and this was an advantage. Finally, several kiwi had been kept in captivity for a number of years so there was knowledge of kiwi husbandry. Despite all the positives, however, much had to be learnt before ONE could be operated on the scale needed to help kiwi.

One of the challenges lay in successful incubation. It was essential to find the right temperature, humidity and turning regime for the huge kiwi egg, and this took some research. Incubation behaviour varies among bird species depending on their ecology and the characteristics of the eggs. When incubation is not done to the specifications for a given species the developing embryo may die or a chick hatch with abnormalities. So for ONE to succeed, we had to learn about kiwi incubation. Rogan Colbourne, the leader of ONE, used 'smart eggs' to gather information about kiwi incubation. Smart eggs are artificial eggs packed with electronics that can log information about temperature and turning. Using them under kiwi of various species, Rogan and his team applied the findings to some trial eggs in captivity. Adjustments were made to suit the conditions, and over the next few years techniques were perfected to the point at which specialists could hatch healthy kiwi chicks.

The next challenge was to raise chicks that could adapt to wild conditions. This is easier said than done: captive-reared animals are not savvy to the ways of the wild and many do not survive once they are released. Nonetheless, we knew from the latest research that above a certain weight (which ranged from 800 g to 1200 g depending, apparently, on location) chicks were able to survive in the presence of stoats, so at least there was an end point to aim for in terms of when it was a good idea to send the chicks back home. Initially, chicks in ONE were kept in captivity until they reached this 'magic' size (at approximately six months old) and then returned to the wild. But they didn't do well, and this failure was attributed to the method of rearing. Accordingly, ONE switched to a strategy of rearing them in a wilder, more natural setting, and looked for predator-free forested sites in which to rear chicks. Chicks grown in these 'kiwi crèches' were better adapted to living in the wild and consequently much more successful when released.

Kiwi sanctuaries

In 1998, the Royal Forest and Bird Protection Society launched 'Kiwis for Kiwis', a conservation campaign that included the creation and maintenance of 11 large areas (10–20,000 ha each) for kiwi recovery. By the year 2000, the government had approved the establishment of five such sanctuaries in key locations earmarked for the most critically endangered kiwi species on the mainland.

To have kiwi survive in wild areas in the mainland it is necessary to get rid of the introduced mammalian predators

Predator control saves kiwis. Traps such as the Fenn trap shown here are deployed throughout kiwi areas.

Improvements to kiwi conservation over the coming years will hopefully see more of these signs appearing in forested areas!

An introduced rat steals poison from a bait station. Left unchecked rats destroy the flowers, fruits and seeds of forest trees, as well as native invertebrates, reptiles, and the eggs and young of many native birds.

that threaten their existence. There are two main ways of doing this: poisoning and trapping. Both techniques are costly to implement and maintain. Poisoning, for example, involves the cost not only of purchasing the poison, but also of delivering it, either by people on foot or by aerial methods. Trapping expenditure includes buying and maintaining traps, and paying trappers. Given that these operations happen in isolated areas of our rugged country, even getting there is usually an expensive exercise. On offshore islands we can eradicate these introduced predators, but it is impossible to do so on the mainland, where, at best, we can reduce predator numbers to a level that allows our native species a degree of breeding success. An added cost now arises, because we must implement a monitoring procedure to measure the success of each operation. This measurement is necessary to determine how often and how intense the operations have to be to achieve the minimum success necessary to allow kiwi to improve their conservation status.

Each of the sanctuaries gave us an opportunity to examine the efficacy of our predator control and monitoring methods. To be able to compare the methods, we needed to collect data on kiwi productivity and dispersal behaviour, which in itself offered a chance to learn more about basic kiwi biology. We also hoped to learn how other native species responded to the control of kiwi predators. This is a very important question because we want to protect all of our native species.

BEECH AND RIMU MASTING

At Haast Kiwi Sanctuary Department of Conservation (DOC) scientists have discovered that regardless of how much trapping for stoats is done, tokoeka chicks end up being eaten. Why does this happen? The forests in this area of New Zealand are mainly of beech interspersed with rimu. Both these tree species are beautiful giants that have a very special breeding strategy. Instead of producing lots of flowers (and therefore fruits and seeds) each year, they produce abnormally high levels of flowers, fruits and seed only every four to six years. In these years, which are called mast years, the bumper yield leads to a superabundance of insects in the forest. Mice and rats, introduced to New Zealand a long time ago, live in the forests and feed on the insects, flowers, fruits and seeds of the beech and rimu. Following the glut, rodent populations explode … and so, too, do the numbers of stoats, whose natural prey is small rodents. However, this all-round boom is followed by an all-round bust: after a mast year comes a poor year, and the insect and rodent populations crash. The stoats, which have bred well with the extra food, are now hungry, and they turn to eat whatever prey is available. Young kiwi, lacking natural defences, are easy prey.

During beech and rimu mast years, mice population increase rapidly …

… following a mast year mice numbers drop. Stoats who had relied on mice for food now turn to native birds such as kereru and kiwi instead.

An initial funding package from the New Zealand Biodiversity Strategy allocated $10 million over five years (2000–05) to the project. Due to the success of these areas in protecting kiwi, the funding of them is now covered within DOC's standard budget. Table 1 below contains information about the kiwi sanctuaries, their aim and outcomes.

Table 1: Kiwi sanctuaries.

Name/ location	Area (ha)	Kiwi species	Management	Results of management regime 2000–10
Whangarei area, Northland	10,000	Brown kiwi	2000–05: stoat trapping; trap checks 30 per year	50–60% of chicks surviving (compared with 11% in non-managed areas) 13% adults increase per year
Moehau/ Kuaotunu, Coromandel	12,000	Brown kiwi	2005–10: reduce trap checks to 12–15 per year	
Tongariro Forest, King Country	15,000	Brown kiwi	2000: 1080 drop ONE	36% of chicks surviving (compared to 12% before poison drop)
South Okarito Forest, West Coast	10,000	Rowi	Stoat trapping in beech forests ONE	Predator control not as successful because of beech and rimu masting (see panel, page 71). ONE better at helping kiwi at these sites than predator control
Haast Range, South Westland	12,000	Haast tokoeka		

Community-based initiatives

Kiwi live all over New Zealand, and not only on DOC land. In fact, many beautiful areas of forest are in private or regional council hands. The various kiwi species require large areas to support healthy and sustainable populations, and managing such areas requires a great deal of commitment and funding. DOC soon realised that, in addition to the five kiwi sanctuaries, they required the help of other landowners in possession of kiwi habitat, and over the last 10 years or so, many community initiatives to save kiwi have been developed. Table 2 below lists these initiatives.

Table 2: Approximate number of community-based projects per area, helping with conserving the various kiwi species in 2010.

Area	Number of projects	Kiwi species
Northland	27	Brown (Northland)
Auckland	9	Brown (Northland) and little spotted kiwi
Coromandel	6	Brown (Coromandel)
Waikato	1	Brown (western)
Bay of Plenty	3	Brown (eastern)
Hawke's Bay	4	Brown (eastern)
East Coast	4	Brown (eastern)
Taranaki	3	Brown (western)
Wanganui and Manawatu	5	Brown (western)
Wellington	2	Brown (eastern and western)
Nelson	3	Great spotted kiwi
West Coast	1	Great spotted kiwi
Canterbury and Christchurch	2	Great spotted kiwi
Total	70	

A community sign in Arthur's Pass township informs tourists of great spotted kiwi in the area.

There are at least 70 kiwi community-based initiatives in New Zealand in 2010 and they are rapidly increasing. According to the DOC website, 60 of those offer protection to kiwi living on 50,000 ha of land. This is in addition to the 70,000 ha protected by DOC for the same purpose. The number of community projects is on the increase, and so the amount of land protected will continue to grow. Most of these projects involve improvements in habitat for kiwi, particularly through predator control, but also through improving the forest and preventing any further land clearance. One of the great spin-offs of such initiatives is that they engage many people who might otherwise not have had the opportunity to help kiwi. In terms of funding, DOC, the Ministry for the Environment, the Department of Internal Affairs, the New Zealand Landcare Trust and the Bank of New Zealand Save the Kiwi Trust, together with many other sources, have all contributed to make these projects a success.

Pure white North Island brown kiwi are very uncommon in the wild. This young female, from Little Barrier Island, is an example of a rare colour abnormality known as leucism.

SPECIES ACCOUNTS

All kiwi species are rounded-looking birds with no visible tail and with strong legs ending in large claws. They have small eyes and large earholes, and have feathers that lack barbules and so have a loose, droopy appearance. The bill is long, slightly curved, and ivory in colour. The base of the bill is surrounded by long whiskers. Males are smaller than females. The wings are very small, ending in a claw that is generally black.

Brown kiwi

Scientific name: *Apteryx mantelli*
Other name: North Island brown kiwi

Identification: The feathers are mostly silvery grey with reddish-brown to black edges, which give the bird its brownish to reddish-black coloration. The apex of the feathers is long, and this creates the impression of hair. Brown kiwi may have completely white feathers interspersed with coloured feathers; birds may have a patch of white in the face, leg or other part of the body, and in some cases all feathers are white (but the bird is not albino). The legs are a reddish grey, and the claws range from white to black. Many birds have half of the claw white and the other half black. Females weigh about 2.8 kg; males about 2 kg.

Distribution: Four taxa are found in parts of the North Island: Coromandel, eastern (kiwi from Bay of Plenty, East Coast, Hawke's Bay), western (kiwi from King Country, Taranaki and Wanganui) and Northland.

Habitat: This species is currently more abundant in lowland and coastal native forests. However, these kiwi also inhabit exotic forest plantations and farmland.

Breeding: Up to two clutches of one or two eggs are laid during May–February. Incubation, undertaken mostly by the male alone, lasts 75.5 ± 5 days. The chick remains in the nest for 25 ± 14 days.

Conservation: The population numbers some 25,000 birds overall but is in serious decline. Of the four genetically distinct groups, the Coromandel kiwi is the only one to be increasing in numbers, thanks to conservation efforts. The other three groups are in decline despite much work done towards increasing populations. In 2008, DOC estimated what kiwi numbers in the different groups would be like in 10 years' time (2018) if conditions remained the same. Under such a scenario, the Northland, eastern and western groups, each with approximately 8000 birds in 2008, were expected to decrease to 6500 apiece. In contrast, the Coromandel kiwi with 1000 birds in 2008 was calculated to increase to 1500 in the same period.

Tokoeka

Haast tokoeka
Scientific name: *Apteryx australis* 'Haast'
Other name: South Island brown kiwi

Identification: The Haast is the smallest of the tokoeka subspecies, with the female weighing 3 kg and the male 2.3 kg.

Distribution: The Haast tokoeka is found in the Haast and Selbourne ranges, and in the Arawhata and Waiatoto river valleys, as well as the Haast Kiwi Sanctuary.

Habitat: It is presumed that the Haast tokoeka is a mountain species because the current highest population densities are found at the bushline in subalpine grasslands (over 1500 metres above sea level) and the base of mountain slopes.

Breeding: A single egg is laid between June and December each year. Both parents take on the task of incubation, which is thought to last around 75 days. The chick nestling period is unknown, but probably matches that of the brown kiwi.

Conservation: The subspecies' status is nationally critical, with a population of just 350, although this is expected to increase to around 600 by 2018.

Fiordland tokoeka
Scientific name: *Apteryx australis*

Identification: In terms of length and weight, this is a medium-sized tokoeka.

Distribution: The subspecies is found exclusively in Fiordland.

Habitat: This subspecies is distributed from the mountains to the sea.

Breeding: A single egg is laid each year between June and December. The parents share the incubation, which is likely to be around 75 days. The nestling period is unknown, but is likely to match that of the brown kiwi.

Conservation: The population of the Fiordland tokoeka, currently totalling some 14,500 birds, is in gradual decline. The northern Fiordland population is expected to fall from 10,000 (2008) to 8500 by 2018, with a corresponding fall from 4500 to 3500 for the southern Fiordland population.

Stewart Island tokoeka
Scientific name: *Apteryx australis lawryi*

Identification: This is the largest of the tokoeka.

Distribution: This subspecies is found all over the island but particularly in the southern two-thirds of Stewart Island.

Habitat: Preferred habitat types are coastal sand dunes, tussock grass, scrub and bush.

Breeding: A single egg is laid each year between June and December. Several members of a group are known to share the incubation, which most likely lasts around 75 days. The chick nestling period is probably as for brown kiwi. After leaving the nest, the young may stay in the family group for several years.

Conservation: The subspecies is in gradual decline, with a population of 15,000 (2008) expected to drop to 12,000 by 2018. It is not well known why the population is in decline, but habitat deterioration has been suggested as the main reason.

Rowi

Scientific name: *Apteryx rowi*
Other names: Okarito kiwi, Okarito brown kiwi

Identification: Males weigh 1.6–2.4 kg; females 2.0–2.5 kg.

Distribution: Okarito Kiwi Sanctuary; small reintroduced population in Blumine Island.

Habitat: Rowi have a single population in the forests of Okarito, on the west coast of the South Island.

Breeding: A single egg is laid each year between June and January. Both parents take part in the incubation, which lasts 65–75 days. The chick nestling period is probably as in brown kiwi, and rowi juveniles can stay in the family group for several years.

Conservation: The rowi's status is nationally critical. The population numbered just 250–350 in 2010, but an increase to around 500 by 2018 is hoped for.

Little spotted kiwi

Scientific name: *Apteryx owenii*
Other name: Kiwi pukupuku

Identification: The feathers are greyish buff with a slight yellowish tone and irregular bands (spots) of earthy brown or brownish black, which give the bird the spotted appearance. In contrast with the great spotted kiwi, little spotted kiwis are much smaller, the legs are pale pinkish-cream, the claws are whitish and the bill is straighter. The body length is 35–45 cm; males weigh 0.9–1.3 kg; females 1–1.9 kg. Male bill length is 63–72 mm; female bill length 75–94 mm.

Distribution: Little spotted kiwi are restricted to Kapiti and other predator-free islands; there is also a small population at Zealandia or Karori Sanctuary, Wellington.

Habitat: On Kapiti Island, little spotted kiwi are most abundant in flax, seral vegetation (see page 43) and older forest. Smaller numbers are found in grassland and scrub.

Breeding: A single egg is laid each year between September and January. The male alone incubates the egg for a period of 65–70 days.

The chick nestling period lasts up to one month; after leaving the nest, the young may stay up to one year in the parents' territory.

Conservation: The little spotted kiwi today has a restricted range, having been eradicated from the mainland by introduced predators. The population currently stands at 1500 or more.

Great spotted kiwi

Scientific name: *Apteryx haastii*
Other names: Roroa, roa

Identification: The feather coloration and pattern are similar to little spotted kiwi, but with a chestnut tinge on the back. The black bands in the feathers are larger and the white ones thinner, giving the bird a darker appearance overall than the little spotted kiwi. Legs are generally greyish with whitish claws. Great spotted kiwi generally come in two colours – a dark, West Coast form lives in wet forests on the western side of the main divide (above), while a paler form lives in alpine zones and east of the main divide (opposite top). Length and weight are 45 cm and 1.2–2.6 kg for the male, 50 cm and 1.5–3.3 kg for the female. Male bill length is 90–100 mm; female 125–135 mm.

Distribution: Great spotted kiwi are found in northwest Nelson, the Paparoa Range and near Arthur's Pass; there is also a translocated population at Rotoiti Mainland Island in Lake Rotoiti, Nelson Lakes National Park.

Habitat: The species is found from sea level to the subalpine zone, but mostly at high altitude areas between 700 and 1000 metres above sea level. Favoured habitats include pasture, tussock grassland, scrub and forest.

Breeding: A single egg is laid each year between July and December. Both parents undertake incubation, which lasts 75–85 days. The chick nestling period is presumed to be the same as that for the brown kiwi.

Conservation: The great spotted kiwi is in gradual decline. Its population, estimated at 16,000 in 2008, is predicted to reduce to 13,000 by 2018.

Pukaha Mount Bruce Wildlife Centre.

WHERE TO SEE KIWI

Kiwi can be seen in many national parks, and farms in Northland and the Coromandel. There are many sites where community projects are caring for kiwi and where there are guided walks.

Wild kiwi:

Kapiti Island
Paraparaumu, Kapiti
+64 6 362 6606
http://kapitiislandnaturetours.co.nz

Karori Wildlife Sanctuary
Karori, Wellington
+ 64 4 920 9200
www.visitzealandia.com

Maungatautari Ecological Island
Karapiro, Waikato
+64 7 823 7455
http://www.maungatrust.org

South Okarito Forest
Westland/Tai Poutini National Park, South Westland
+ 64 3 756 9100
westcoast@doc.govt.nz

Stewart Island
Stewart Island/Rakiura; transport from the mainland is by fixed-wing aircraft, helicopter or ferry
+ 64 3 219 1049
www.stewartisland.co.nz

Tiritiri Matangi Island
Hauraki Gulf (ferries from Gulf Harbour on the Whangaparaoa Peninsula, and from central Auckland)
0800 Discovery/+ 64 9 424 5510
www.360discovery.co.nz

Trounson Kauri Park
SH 12, near Dargaville, Northland
+ 64 9 439 3450
kauricoastareaoffice@doc.govt.nz

Captive kiwi:
Auckland Zoo
Western Springs, Auckland
+64 9 360 3805
www.aucklandzoo.co.nz

Kiwi Birdlife Park
Queenstown
+ 64 3 442 8059
www.kiwibird.co.nz

Kiwi Encounter
Rainbow Springs Kiwi Wildlife Park,
Rotorua
0800 724 626/+ 64 7 350 0440
www.rainbowsprings.co.nz

National Kiwi Centre
Hokitika, West Coast
+64 3 755 5251
www.thenationalkiwicentre.co.nz

Nga Manu Nature Reserve
Waikanae
+64 4 293 4131
www.ngamanu.co.nz

Orana Wildlife Park and Southern
Encounter Aquarium and Kiwi House
Christchurch
+64 3 359 7109
www.southernencounter.co.nz

Otorohanga Kiwi House
Otorohanga, Waikato
+64 7 873 7391
www.kiwihouse.org.nz

Pukaha Mt Bruce National Wildlife
Centre
SH2, between Eketahuna and Masterton
+ 64 6 375 8004
www.mtbruce.org.nz

Te Puia Kiwi Conservation Centre
Te Puia, Rotorua
0800 83 7842/+64 7 348 9047
www.tepuia.com

Wellington Zoo
Newtown, Wellington
+64 4 389 3692
www.wellingtonzoo.com

West Coast Wildlife Centre
Franz Josef
+64 3 752 0600
www.wildkiwi.co.nz

Whangarei Museum and Heritage Park
Whangarei
+64 9 438 9630
www.whangareimuseum.co.nz

Willowbank Wildlife Reserve
Christchurch
+64 3 359 6226
www.willowbank.co.nz

Beech forest in the Arthur Valley, Fiordland.

GLOSSARY

Cloaca (vent)
A single opening in the body of a bird or a reptile, where the intestinal, genital and urinary tracts all terminate. When mating, two individuals place their cloaca in contact so that sperm passes from the male to the female.

Gondwana
This was the southern part of the Pangaea supercontinent, which about 250 million years ago comprised all of the world's land masses (now broken into separate continents). Gondwana drifted away from Laurasia, the northern part of Pangaea, 200–180 million years ago. New Zealand and its parent land mass, Australia, formed a part of Gondwana.

K-Pg Boundary
The point in geological time marking the close of the Cretaceous Period (136–65 million years ago) and the start of the Paleogene Period (65–23 million years ago). The Paleogene witnessed the rise of the mammals.

Neognathae
One of the two main superorders of birds. Neognaths have a 'bird palate', as opposed to a palate resembling that of a reptile. See also *Palaeognathae*.

Palaeognathae
One of the two main superorders of birds. Palaeognaths (which include kiwi) have a palate that resembles that of reptiles. They also have a flat sternum, usually without a keel, and show poor flying ability or are flightless. See also *Neognathae*.

Ratite
A collective term, increasingly considered out of date, for a flightless bird – e.g. an ostrich, emu or moa.

Sex role reversal
A behaviour in which a father takes on the traditional role of the mother.

Theropod
A dinosaur of the suborder Theropoda, characterised by a lizard-style arrangement of the hip bones and by a two-legged gait. The term 'theropod' is also applied to birds, the modern descendants of these dinosaurs.

North Island brown kiwi.

FURTHER READING AND BIBLIOGRAPHY

The main source of information for this book comes from 110 scientific publications produced by large number of scientists, and spanning 120 years (the first one was written in 1891 and the last one 2011). In addition, a lot of information on kiwi is contained in reports either requested by or carried out by Department of Conservation (DOC) personnel, so I used information from 13 of those. Much information about kiwi is also contained in theses written by Masters and PhD students and I have used information from 11 of them.

So, there isn't space here to list all sources I have drawn on for this book, but I would especially like to acknowledge the following people, whose research papers have been instrumental: Rogan Colbourne and collaborators particularly Hugh Robertson, Jim Jolly, Marian Burbridge, and Ruud Kleinpaste; John McLennan and collaborators particularly Britta Basse and Murray Potter. The following graduate students: Lee Shapiro, Susan Cunningham, Birgit Ziesseman, Jeremy Corfield, Julia Latham, Carryn Hojem, Charlotte Minson, Yuri Forbes, Cindy Jenkins, and Jonathan Miles for the use of their theses. Figure 2 was made based mostly on a figure from M.J. Phillips and collaborators, but I included information on papers from: J. Cracraft and collaborators, O. Hadrath and collaborators, J. Harshman and collaborators, and A. Cooper and collaborators.

If you would like to receive a full reference list please contact me via email at: i.c.castro@massey.ac.nz

Bibliography

Websites

http://www.kiwirecovery.org.nz/
http://people.eku.edu/ritchisong/ornitholsyl.htm
http://www.doc.govt.nz/

Posters and Fact sheets

(Available through the Department of Conservation website under Publications)

Colbourne, R., Van Klink, P., Hieatt, M., Lyall, J. 2001 Pamphlet. *Haast Tokoeka: mountain kiwi on the edge*, New Zealand Department of Conservation, Wellington.

Department of Conservation. 2010 Pamphlet. *Rowi: the rarest of them all*, New Zealand Department of Conservation, Hokitika.

Scientific papers from Journals

(Available through some libraries especially university libraries)

Baker, A.J., Daugherty, C.H., Colbourne, R., McLennan, J.L. 1995. Flightless brown kiwis of New Zealand possess extremely subdivided population structure and cryptic species like small mammals. *Proceedings of the National Academy of Sciences of the United States of America*, 92: 8254–8258.

Berry, C. 1999. Potential interactions of hedgehogs with North Island brown kiwi at Boundary Stream Mainland Island. In *Conservation Advisory Science Notes No. 268*. Wellington, New Zealand Department of Conservation. 22 pp-.

Corfield, J.R. 2009. Evolution of the brain and sensory systems of the kiwi. PhD Thesis. University of Auckland, Auckland.

Cunningham, S.J. 2006. Foraging sign, prey detection and bill morphology in the North Island brown kiwi (*Apteryx mantelli*). BSc Honours thesis. Massey University, Palmerston North.

Cunningham, S.J. 2010. Tactile senses and foraging in birds, with emphasis on kiwi. PhD thesis. Massey University, Palmerston North.

McLennan, J.A. 1988. Breeding of North Island brown kiwi, *Apteryx australis mantelli*, in Hawkes Bay, New Zealand. *New Zealand Journal of Ecology*, 11: 89–97.

McLennan, J.A., Potter, M.A., Robertson, H.A., Wake, G.C., Colbourne, R., Dew, L., Joyce, L., McCann, A.J., Miles, J., Miller, P.J., Reid, J. 1996. Role of predation in the decline of kiwi, *Apteryx* spp, in New Zealand. *New Zealand Journal of Ecology*, 20: 27–35.

Potter, M.A. 1990. Movement of North Island brown kiwi (*Apteryx australis mantelli*) between forest remnants. *New Zealand Journal of Ecology*, 14: 17–24.

Taborsky, B., Taborsky, M. 1992. Spatial-organization of the North Island brown kiwi *Apteryx australis mantelli* – sex, pairing status and territoriality. *Ibis*, 134: 1–10.

Ziesemann, B. 2011. Social organisation and mating system of a high-density brown kiwi (*Apteryx mantelli*) population. PhD thesis. Massey University, Auckland.

Mixed beech and podocarp forest, Haast.

ACKNOWLEDGEMENTS

IC: I would like to thank my students and postdocs, in particular; Susan Cunningham, Birgit Ziesseman, Alex Wilson and Sarah Jamieson, for their comments on earlier drafts of this book. You guys are inspiring and motivate me to keep going. Thanks also to Steve Trewick, Rogan Colbourne and John McLennan for critically reading the text and thus improving its content. I am also indebted to many people and organisations for their role in various aspects of my kiwi research: in particular, Susanna Brow, Dave and Ros Chamberlin, and Pete and Pat Chamberlin, as well as Massey University for their unwavering support over the last seven years.

RM: The photographs in this book would not have been possible without the Department of Conservation staff at Arthur's Pass, Christchurch, Franz Josef, and Te Anau, and the staff at Otorohanga Kiwi House, Maungatautari Trust, and at Willowbank Wildlife Reserve. Also thanks to Bevan and Lorraine Alexander, Rachel Anson, Jane Arrow, Tony Billing and Bronwyn Buckley, Ieuan Davies, Pat Follas, Dominique Fortis, Eric Fox, Nicola Hansen, Duncan Kaye, Mark Lammas, Corry-Ann Langford, Jim Livingston, Jeremy McGuire, Nic Menary, Melanie Nelson, Barry Rowe, Phillip and Diane Smith, Chris Smuts-Kennedy, Jane Tansell, and Michael Willis.

Dr Jim Mills and Don Merton provided my early opportunities to watch kiwi – southern tokoeka – living untroubled lives in Fiordland. Thank you to DOC field staff and volunteers everywhere, who strive to keep it that way for kiwi today.

Podocarp forest at sunset, Haast.

INDEX

Also from New Holland Publishers

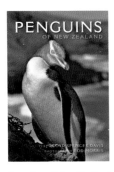

Penguins of New Zealand
978 1 86966 261 5

A Photographic Guide to
Birds of New Zealand
(second edition)
978 1 86966 327 8

New Zealand Bird Calls
978 1 86966 310 0

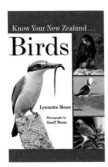

Know Your New Zealand
Birds
978 1 86966 089 5

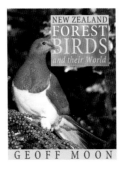

New Zealand Forest Birds
and their World
978 1 86966 196 0

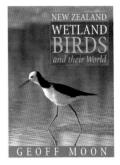

New Zealand Wetland Birds
and their World
978 1 86966 197 7

Where to Watch Birds in
New Zealand
978 1 86966 154 0

Birds of New Zealand
978 1 86966 333 9

Birds of New Zealand
Checklist
978 1 86966 119 9